VEGAN
MEETS
TURKISH KITCHEN

Seda Dayioglu

ISBN: 978-1-7770099-0-8 (Paperback)

First paperback edition November 2019.

SD International Inc.
11227 162A Avenue
Edmonton, AB
Canada
T5X 1Z9

DEDICATION

TO ALL THE COMPASSIONATE PEOPLE.
THOSE WHO,
OUT OF COMPASSION FOR THE ANIMALS,
OUT OF COMPASSION FOR THE ENVIRONMENT,
AND EVEN COMPASSION FOR THEMSELVES
CHOOSE TO EAT VEGAN.

TABLE OF CONTENTS

SALADS   35

MAIN DISHES & SIDES   43

ACKNOWLEDGMENTS

A BIG THANK YOU GOES OUT TO
MY GRANDMA, MY MOM, AND MY AUNT
FOR TEACHING ME THESE RECIPES.
THANKS TO THEM I AM ABLE TO SHARE THEM
WITH YOU.

I WOULD ALSO LIKE TO THANK
YOU FOR PICKING UP THIS BOOK!

FOREWORD

Welcome to the vegan side of the Turkish kitchen! I'm Seda and I have been living vegan for many years, enjoying all this lifestyle has to offer. Coming from a Turkish background, however, had its own challenges, especially when it came to family. When my family first found out that I became vegan they were not impressed. Whether it is a nicely grilled kebab, tripe soup, or feta cheese, Turkish meals always have a contribution from the animal kingdom. In the beginning not only my mom was wondering what to cook for me when I came over, I, too, asked myself if there was any Turkish food left to eat as a vegan. I quickly realized that not only are there a lot of Turkish dishes that can be made vegan, but many are naturally vegan besides.

Baked goods like pita bread or pastry play an important role in the Turkish kitchen. Many recipes ask for milk or butter and one theoretically could substitute these with vegan alternatives. This will not be necessary, however, because 90% of the recipes in this cookbook are 100% vegan. On rare occasions you will be asked to use vegan yogurt, for example. In other words, you will hardly find a recipe that has been jazzed up or changed from its original form. For the most part you will find Turkish classics that my grandma made the way she learned from her grandma.

A Mediterranean kitchen without olive oil is not a Mediterranean kitchen and the Turks use a lot of it. But if

1

you want to reduce your oil intake or stay away from it altogether, you can fry with water or steam. It's different and it might not taste as good as with a fine olive oil.

There is a whole palette of tasty cold dishes that are prepared with olive oil. The so called *Zeytinyağlılar* have a special place not only in every Turkish buffet but also in this cookbook. Generally eaten after the main dish and especially in summer when the days are hot, these cold dishes have a refreshing charm after your main course.

You will notice that many recipes ask for onions, tomato paste, and red pepper paste. These are staple ingredients and contribute immensely to the dish's flavor. Other important ingredients are parsley, dried mint, and lemon juice. The latter is even used in some desserts.

Then there are a variety of vegetable dishes that are prepared depending on what the season has to offer and the availability in the region. The Turkish climate is ideal for many types of vegetables to be grown and therefore the use of these fresh ingredients is common. It is also easy to get these ingredients in other countries — mostly thanks to Turkish (and non-Turkish) immigrants who ride the wave of globalization, opening cultural food stores and thereby a gateway to nonlocal ingredients. You might have to go to a Turkish supermarket or other ethnic grocery store to get some staple ingredients that are listed in this book.

I placed the Turkish name of the ingredients in brackets so please shop accordingly. Bulgur has a fine and coarse distinction and each type is used differently. The unique types of pepper mentioned in this book, although similar, are not interchangeable (refer to page 34 and 41 for differentiation) and cannot be replaced with bell pepper, for example. The red pepper paste should not be confused with Harissa or Korean Gochujang red pepper paste. The pumpkin mentioned on page 74 cooks and tastes differently than other types of pumpkin. Therefore it is important that you buy the exact ingredients as mentioned in the brackets!

It is also worth mentioning that the Turkish kitchen offers a variety of dishes with beans and other legumes. Legumes are high in protein, reducing or replacing the amount of animal protein in the Mediterranean diet. They keep you feeling satiated longer, are inexpensive, and sustainable.

If you are familiar with the Turkish kitchen, then you know that the desserts can get really sweet. Nowadays it is easier to reach for sugar alternatives that did not exist in my grandma's time. Stevia is my personal favorite because it can substitute sugar very well. If you want to pass on refined sugar but not on dessert, you have some choices.

It is with great pleasure that I give you these classic recipes that were passed on to me by my grandma, mum, and auntie. I hope you will like them and that you enjoy eating plant based, Turkish style. Keep in mind that a Turkish meal is perfectly topped off with a glass of Turkish black tea or a cup of Turkish coffee.

Enjoy! Or as we say in Turkish, *Afiyet olsun!*
Sincerely yours, *Seda*

Turkish black tea – *çay*

Turkish coffee - *türk kahvesi*

APPETIZERS, FINGER FOODS & SNACKS

STUFFED GRAPE LEAVES – *Yaprak Sarma*

Serves 4-6

Prep time: 1½ hours

Difficulty level: moderate

Cooking time: 1 hour

INGREDIENTS

1 pkg (17.6 oz/500 g)	pickled grape leaves
1½ cups (350 g)	rice
2	onions, medium sized
2-3	garlic cloves
	olive oil
2 Tbsp	red pepper paste, sweet (*tatlı biber salçası*)
1 tsp	dried mint
	hot red pepper flakes (*pul biber*)
	salt
	pepper
1	lemon
	water

DIRECTIONS

Wash grape leaves thoroughly and let them sit in lukewarm water for at least half an hour. Change the water once during this process. Wash the rice, rinse and put aside.

Finely chop onions and garlic. In a saucepan, sauté onions and garlic in 3 Tbsp of olive oil on high heat for a minute. Add red pepper paste and washed rice and continue sautéing for another 5 minutes or until onions are soft, stirring frequently. Remove saucepan from heat and add dried mint. If you like it spicy, add hot red pepper flakes to the rice mixture now. Add salt and pepper but show restraint when using salt since the pickled grape leaves are already salty.

Remove and discard bigger stems from the grape leaves and put aside damaged leaves. Place leaf flat with its shiny side down and the pointy tip away from you. Put one heaping teaspoon of the rice mixture horizontally at the bottom stem part of the leaf, fold sides towards the middle and roll up to the pointy tip, making a nice looking roll. Make the roll neither too tight nor too loose. Amount of mixture will vary with size of leaf. Repeat for each leaf.

Place rolls into a high pot, making layers as you go up, leaving no gaps. After each layer is complete, drizzle some olive oil. Put a few lemon slices on the last layer of rolls.
Extra weight is needed on the rolls to prevent them from opening during cooking. Take a flat dinner plate that will fit into the pot and place it face down on the rolls. Fill the pot with hot water up to the plate, cover with lid and bring to a boil. Turn down and simmer over medium heat for 60 minutes or until rice is cooked. Remove from heat, let cool, and serve warm or cold.

RED LENTIL PATTIES – *Mercimek Köftesi*

Serves 5-6

Difficulty level: easy

Prep time: 10 minutes

Cooking time: 40 minutes

INGREDIENTS

1 cup (200 g)	red lentils
2½ cups (625 ml)	hot water
1 tsp	salt
1 cup (225 g)	fine bulgur (*köftelik ince bulgur*)
½ cup (100 ml)	olive oil
1	onion, large, finely chopped
1½ tsp	tomato paste
1 tsp	pepper paste, sweet (*tatlı biber salçası*)
	juice of a lemon
1 tsp	cumin, ground
1 tsp	sweet paprika, ground
4	green onions, chopped
½ bunch	fresh parsley, finely chopped
	romaine lettuce leaves to serve on

DIRECTIONS

Wash red lentils thoroughly, preferably in a colander to check for stones. In a saucepan combine lentils, hot water, and salt. Cook over medium to low heat for about 20 minutes or until most of the water is absorbed.

Stir lentils and add the bulgur, mixing well. Cover and put aside for 10–15 minutes or until the bulgur is very soft.

In a skillet heat a quarter cup (50 ml) of oil, add chopped onion and sauté until soft. Add tomato paste and red pepper paste, mix well and cook for another minute.

Put lentil and bulgur mixture together with the sautéed onion into a mixing bowl. Add the juice of a whole lemon, the remainder of the olive oil, cumin, and paprika and mix well. Add finely chopped green onions and parsley and mix gently.

Line a serving platter with romaine lettuce leaves. With wet hands, form oval shaped lentil patties. Place patties on lettuce leaves and serve cold. The perfect snack or finger food.

Afiyet olsun!

CRISPY ROLLS – *Sigara Böreği*

Serves 4-5

Difficulty level: easy

Prep time: 10-20 minutes

Cooking time: 30-40 minutes

INGREDIENTS

5-6	potatoes, medium-sized, waxy
	water
	salt
	oil
2	onions, medium-sized, chopped
1 tsp	paprika, sweet, ground
	hot red pepper flakes (*pul biber*)
1 pkg	triangle pastry leaves (*yufka*), usually comes in 13 oz (360 g) packages

DIRECTIONS

Peel and wash potatoes. Cut into cubes and cook in salted water for about 20 minutes. Drain water and mash potatoes.

In a medium-sized skillet, heat oil and sauté onions until soft. Add paprika, hot red pepper flakes to your liking, and the mashed potatoes. Mix well with the onions and cook for another 5 minutes. Salt to taste.

Place pastry triangles on a flat surface with the tip pointing away from you. Spread some potato mixture onto the wide side of the triangle closest to you. Fold both side corners to the center and roll the triangle up to the tip.

To prevent the roll from opening, wet the point of the triangle with water before you roll it up completely. The water makes the tip sticky, so make sure you have a small cup of water ready beside you when preparing the rolls.

Heat oil in a large skillet and fry the rolls on all sides until golden brown. Put the rolls on paper towel after frying so that the excess oil gets absorbed. Serve hot as an appetizer with tea.

Afiyet olsun!

RAW BULGUR PATTIES – *Çiğ Köfte*

Serves 4-6

Difficulty level: moderate

Prep time: 30-40 minutes

Resting time: 10 minutes

INGREDIENTS

1⅜ cups (300 g)	fine bulgur (*köftelik ince bulgur*)
	hot water
2	onions, medium-sized, grated
4 Tbsp	fresh parsley, finely chopped
2 Tbsp	tomato paste
2 Tbsp	red pepper paste, sweet (*tatlı biber salçası*)
1 tsp	paprika, sweet, ground
2 Tbsp	olive oil
1 Tbsp	pomegranate molasses (*nar ekşisi*)
2 Tbsp	lemon juice
	salt and pepper
	lettuce leaves to serve on, romaine or iceberg

DIRECTIONS

Put bulgur in a container and immerse it almost completely with hot water. Let it rest, covered for at least 10 minutes, until all the water is absorbed by the bulgur.

Peel and grate onions. Place them in a strainer and hold them under running water to get rid of the onion juice. This step prevents the patties from tasting bitter.

Combine all ingredients – except lettuce leaves, pomegranate molasses, and lemon juice – in a mixing bowl. Add bulgur and knead well for 20–30 minutes. Alternatively, you can use a kneading machine or dough mixer to spare you this task.

Çiğ Köfte is traditionally eaten spicy. If you like spicy food, then add 1 tsp of hot red pepper flakes (*pul biber*) before mixing.

Dip your hands in cold water, take a walnut sized lump and squeeze lightly in your palm to give it a typical shape as seen in the picture. Place patties on a serving plate and sprinkle them with lemon juice and/or pomegranate molasses. Wrap them with lettuce leaves and enjoy.

Afiyet olsun!

CRISPY BAGELS – *Simit*

Makes 6 bagels

Prep time: 20-30 minutes

Baking time: 15-20 minutes

Difficulty level: easy

Rising time: 20-40 minutes

DOUGH INGREDIENTS

1 tsp	dry yeast, dissolved in warm water
3¼ cups (400 g)	flour
1 tsp	salt
1¾ cups (400 ml)	lukewarm water

GLAZE INGREDIENTS

1 cup (150 g)	raw sesame seeds, dried
4 Tbsp	grape syrup (*pekmez*, or any molasses)
½ cup (100 ml)	water
1 Tbsp	flour

DIRECTIONS

Dissolve dry yeast in lukewarm water, according to package instructions and set aside for about 5 minutes.

To make the dough, pour yeast into a bowl along with flour, salt, and lukewarm water. Mix until a nice doughy texture develops, sprinkling flour if too sticky, water if too dry, until perfect. Knead thoroughly to get a nice, smooth dough. Remove the ball of dough, sprinkle flour into the bowl and place the dough back in. Cover with a kitchen towel and put in a warm place for 20-40 minutes, until the dough doubles in size.

In the meantime, roast sesame seeds in a frying pan until

golden brown. No oil is needed for this process. It is normal for the sesame seeds to jump up from the heat. Put the roasted sesame into a bowl.

Make the glaze in a separate bowl. Mix grape syrup, water, and flour together and set aside. Preheat oven to 450°F (230°C).

Sprinkle flour on a flat working surface. Once the dough is ready, put it on the flat working surface and divide into 12 equally sized pieces. With your hands, form the pieces into balls, then, still with your hands, roll them into long strings half an inch (1 cm) thick. Lay two strings parallel to each other, then twist the strings around each other a few times until the two lengths are completely wrapped around each other. Form a circle by connecting the ends, the outer diameter should be between four and six inches (10–15 cm).

Dip the ring into the syrup mix first, then dab all sides in the sesame bowl, covering the ring with sesame. Place on a baking sheet lined with parchment paper. Repeat for all. Put the baking sheet on the middle rack and place a casserole dish filled with water right underneath on the lower rack. The water causes the simit to become crispy. Bake for 15 to 20 minutes or until golden brown.

TURKISH PIZZA – *Lahmacun*

Makes 8 pizzas

Prep time: 20 minutes

Cooking time: 10 minutes

Difficulty level: easy

Rising time: 30 minutes

Baking time: 30–40 minutes

DOUGH INGREDIENTS

3¼ cups (400 g)	flour
1 tsp	fresh yeast
1 tsp	salt
1 Tbsp	olive oil
1⅞ cups (200 ml)	warm water

TOPPING INGREDIENTS

⅜ cup (50 g)	walnuts, finely chopped
2	onions, large-sized, finely chopped
1	red bell pepper, finely chopped
3 Tbsp	oil for frying
2¼ cups (500 ml)	tomato puree
2 Tbsp	tomato paste
1 Tbsp	pepper paste, sweet (*tatlı biber salçası*)
1 Tbsp	sesame seeds
½ Tbsp	thyme
½ Tbsp	dried mint
1 tsp	cumin, ground
1 tsp	salt
½ tsp	pepper
	hot red pepper flakes (*pul biber*) to taste

DIRECTIONS

In a mixing bowl add flour, fresh yeast, salt, and oil. Gradually add warm water to dissolve yeast and knead thoroughly to form a dough. Cover and let dough rise in a warm place for about 30 minutes.

Heat oil in a frying pan, add onions and sauté for 2 minutes or until soft. Add bell pepper and cook for another 2 minutes. Add the rest of the topping ingredients and cook for 5 minutes.

Preheat oven to 460°F (240°C). Divide dough into 8 pieces and form balls. On a floured surface roll out the balls into thin round or oval shapes using a rolling pin. Place 2 to 4 pieces of flat dough onto a baking sheet lined with parchment paper.

Spread topping evenly over each piece of dough and bake on the middle rack for 5-10 minutes or until the edges of the pizzas are golden brown.

Cover the cooked pizzas with a clean kitchen towel so that they do not dry out while the other pizzas are still in the oven. One can eat them warm, just like this but...

An optional serving suggestion which many Turks enjoy is to roll the pizzas up with salad filling. Make the filling out of chopped iceberg lettuce, tomatoes, cucumbers and onions tossed in olive oil. Place salad filling onto pizzas and roll them up. Alternatively, you can sprinkle pizzas with some lemon juice and garnish with fresh parsley.

TURKISH PITA BREAD – *Pide*

Serves 4-6

Prep time: 15-20 minutes

Baking time: 20-30 minutes

Difficulty level: easy

Resting time: about 1½ hours

INGREDIENTS

2 Tbsp	fresh yeast
4 cups (500 g)	flour
1½ tsp	salt
½ tsp	sugar
3 Tbsp	olive oil
1½ cups (375 ml)	water
	sesame seeds
	black cumin seeds

DIRECTIONS

In a large mixing bowl add flour, salt, sugar, olive oil, yeast, and water. Dissolve yeast and knead thoroughly until dough is soft. Cover dough and let sit in a warm place for about 40 minutes.

Knead dough again, cover and let rest in a warm place for another 20 minutes.

Line baking sheet with parchment paper. Oil hands and place the soft dough onto baking sheet. Oiling prevents the dough from sticking to hands. Give dough a round shape and flatten slightly. With a knife cut a raster onto the dough.

Lightly wet top of dough with water and sprinkle with sesame seeds and black cumin seeds, making them stick.

Preheat oven to 430°F (220°C). Let dough rise on the baking sheet until it doubles its size.

Bake for 20-30 minutes or until golden brown.

Afiyet olsun!

BUNS – *Poğaça*

Serves 6-8

Prep time: 10-15 minutes

Baking time: 15-20 minutes

Difficulty level: easy

Resting time: 45 minutes

DOUGH INGREDIENTS

1 Tbsp	dry yeast
1¾ cup (400 ml)	warm water
2 tsp	sugar
½ cup (100 ml)	oil
4 cups (500 g)	flour

FOR THE GLAZE

1 Tbsp	grape syrup (*pekmez* or any other type of molasses)
1 Tbsp	water
	sesame seeds
	black cumin seeds

DIRECTIONS

Dissolve yeast in a glass with ⅞ cup (200 ml) of water, add 1 tsp of sugar and mix well. Place glass in a mixing bowl in case of overflow. Wait 15 minutes. Then pour glass contents into the mixing bowl and add oil, ⅞ cup (200 ml) water, and 1 tsp of sugar. Gradually add flour to the bowl and knead until you get a soft dough. Add flour as needed in order to prevent the dough from sticking to fingers. Cover dough and let rise in a warm place for about 30 minutes.

Preheat oven to 360°F (180°C). Form oval shaped balls slightly larger than an egg and flatten slightly. Place them on a baking sheet lined with parchment paper.

Mix grape syrup with water until consistent. Brush onto balls. Sprinkle balls with sesame and black cumin seeds.

Bake for 15 to 20 minutes or until golden brown.

These buns go well with salads. You can also cut them in half and put your favorite spread on them. A traditional option would be to bake them with filling like potatoes (page 11) or spinach (page 25).

Afiyet olsun!

SPREAD – E*z*me

Serves 4-6

Difficulty level: easy

Prep time: 10 minutes

Resting time: 1 hour

INGREDIENTS

4	tomatoes, medium-sized
¼ bunch	fresh parsley, finely chopped
4	green onions, finely chopped
2	garlic cloves
½ Tbsp	tomato paste
½ Tbsp	red pepper paste (*tatlı biber salçası*)
3 Tbsp	olive oil
	juice of a lemon
½ tsp	salt
1 tsp	dried mint
1 tsp	hot red pepper flakes (*pul biber*)

DIRECTIONS

Peel and dice tomatoes.

Wash parsley and green onions, drain and chop.

Peel garlic cloves and either dice or grate or press.

Mix tomato paste with red pepper paste, adding oil and lemon juice.

Add all ingredients into a mixing bowl, mix well and mash with a fork. Let sit for about an hour.

This spread goes well with the buns on page 20 or the Turkish pita bread on page 18.

You can adjust the spiciness to taste. If you like it spicier then you can add more hot red pepper flakes.

Afiyet olsun!

FILLED FLATBREAD – *Gözleme*

Makes 12 flatbreads

Prep time: 15-20 minutes

Frying time: 20-30 minutes

Difficulty level: easy

Resting time: 30 minutes

Foto by foodiesfeed / Freepik

INGREDIENTS

1¼ cups (150 g)	flour
2 tsp	salt
½ cup (100 ml)	warm water
14.1 oz (400 g)	fresh spinach leaves
1	onion, large-sized
	oil
	black pepper
	hot red pepper flakes (*pul biber*) to taste

DIRECTIONS

Add flour, 1 tsp of salt, and water to a mixing bowl and knead until you get a soft dough. Add more flour if needed to prevent the dough from sticking on hands. Roll the dough into a log. Cut dough into 12 pieces and roll into balls. Place balls onto a floured surface and cover with a damp kitchen towel. Let rest for about 30 minutes.

Wash spinach thoroughly, drain, and cut into very fine strips. Peel and dice onion. In a frying pan heat 3 Tbsp of oil and sauté onion until soft. Add 1 tsp of salt, pepper, and hot red pepper flakes to taste.

In a mixing bowl combine sautéed onion and spinach.

On a floured surface roll out the balls into thin round shapes using a rolling pin. The diameter should be around eight inches (20 cm). Spread the onion-spinach mixture onto half of the round shape, leaving a border around the edge so when you fold the other half over, the dough edges can seal together with a light pinch.

Heat oil in a frying pan on medium heat. Fry flatbread for 2½ minutes on each side or until golden brown.

Afiyet olsun!

CORNBREAD – *Mısır Ekmeği*

Serves 4-6

Prep time: 10 minutes

Difficulty level: easy

Baking time: 40-60 minutes

INGREDIENTS

2⅞ cups (360 g)	corn flour
1 tsp	dry yeast
1 tsp	salt
1 tsp	sugar
3½ Tbsp	oil + more to grease pan
1¾ cups (400 ml)	warm water

DIRECTIONS

Preheat oven to 360°F (180°C). To a mixing bowl add corn flour, dry yeast, salt, sugar, and oil. Mix well. Gradually add warm water to form a batter.

Pour the batter evenly into a greased nonstick skillet, casserole dish (round or square), or any other bakeware of your choice.

Bake bread for 40-50 minutes or until crust is light brown. The bread should not be too dry; therefore, it is recommended to adjust upper and lower heat accordingly.

Cornbread is a staple food of the black sea region and is traditionally eaten with soups or yogurt. It can be made in batches and frozen for later, too.

SOUPS

YELLOW LENTIL SOUP – *Sarı Mercimek Çorbası*

Serves 2-4

Prep time: 10-15 minutes

Difficulty level: easy

Cooking time: 30 minutes

INGREDIENTS

⅞ cup (170 g)	yellow lentils
1	carrot
1	onion, large-sized
4 Tbsp	oil
2 Tbsp	flour
4¼ cups (1 L)	water or vegetable stock
	salt
	dried mint
	hot red pepper flakes (*pul biber*)

DIRECTIONS

Wash yellow lentils thoroughly to remove dirt and starch. Drain and set aside.

Peel and dice carrot and onion.

In a saucepot, heat 2 Tbsp of oil, sauté onion and carrot until soft. Add 2 Tbsp of oil and flour into the same saucepot to make a roux. Add yellow lentils and water (or vegetable stock).

Salt to taste and stir until boiling. Cover and let simmer on medium heat for 20-25 minutes.

Smooth with a hand blender and serve with dried mint and hot red pepper flakes.

The soup thickens over time. Simply add a little bit of water before heating next time.

Afiyet olsun!

RED LENTIL SOUP – *Kırmızı Mercimek Çorbası*

Serves 4-6

Prep time: 10 minutes

Difficulty level: easy

Cooking time: about. 40 minutes

INGREDIENTS

1½ cups (300 g)	red lentils
1	onion, large-sized
1	garlic clove
2	potatoes, medium-sized
1	carrot
3 Tbsp	oil
6⅜ cups (1½ L)	hot water
	salt
	pepper
1 tsp	dried mint
	lemon juice

DIRECTIONS

Wash red lentils thoroughly, drain and set aside.

Peel onion and garlic clove. Dice onion and mince garlic. Peel potatoes and carrot. Wash and dice these as well.

In a saucepan heat oil, sauté onion and garlic until soft.

Add carrot and red lentils, stir for a few seconds. Pour hot water into the pot and stir again.
Add potatoes and stir. Cover and cook on medium heat for 30 minutes. Add salt and pepper to taste.

Use hand blender to smooth and add 1 tsp of dried mint.

Serve hot with a spritz of lemon juice and some fresh pita bread (page 18). For more spiciness add some hot red pepper flakes.

If you make this soup in a pressure cooker, the cooking time goes down to about 15 minutes.

Afiyet olsun!

VILLAGE SOUP – *Köy Çorbası*

Serves 4-6
Prep time: 10-20 minutes
Cooking time: 40-50 minutes

Difficulty level: moderate
Resting time: 8-10 hours

INGREDIENTS

½ cup (100 g)	black-eyed peas (*börülce*)
¾ cup (150 g)	green lentils
2	onions, medium-sized
6 Tbsp	oil
1 Tbsp	tomato paste
6⅜ cups (1½ L)	hot water + more to precook
3 Tbsp	rice
2 Tbsp	risoni/orzo or capellini tagliati (*arpa şehriye* or *tel şehriye*)
1 Tbsp	dried purple basil (*reyhan*)
	salt and pepper

risoni/orzo – *arpa şehriye*:
short-cut, rice-shaped pasta

capellini tagliati - *tel şehriye*:
short-cut, vermicelli-like pasta

DIRECTIONS

Wash black-eyed peas and green lentils separately yet thoroughly. Let them soak in water overnight in separate bowls.

In a pot boil water, add drained lentils and peas. Cook for 10 minutes. Discard the cooking water to prevent the soup from getting too dark.

Wash and drain rice and set aside.

Peel and dice onions. Add 5 Tbsp of oil to a pot and sauté onions until soft. Add tomato paste, black-eyed peas and green lentils. Pour in 6⅜ cups (1½ L) of hot water, stir well, and bring to a boil.

Add rice and risoni/orzo (or vermicelli) to the pot. Cover and let simmer on low heat for 30-40 minutes. Stir occasionally and check the water level. If the soup gets too thick, simply add more water. If you prepare the soup in a pressure cooker, then the cooking time will be cut down to approximately 15 minutes.

In a saucepan sauté dried purple basil in 1 Tbsp of oil for a minute and combine with the soup. Add salt and pepper to taste.

The soup thickens over time. Simply add a little bit of water before heating next time.

Afiyet olsun!

TOMATO SOUP – *Domates Çorbası*

Serves 2-4

Prep time: 10 minutes

Difficulty level: easy

Cooking time: 20 minutes

INGREDIENTS

1	onion
2	tomatoes, large-sized, peeled
2	sweet banana peppers, green (*çarliston biberi*)
1	carrot
2 Tbsp	oil
2 Tbsp	tomato paste
3⅜ cups (800 ml)	vegetable stock
2-3 Tbsp	rice
	salt and pepper
½ tsp	sugar
a handful	fresh parsley

DIRECTIONS

Peel onion and tomatoes. Finely dice onion, tomatoes, and sweet banana peppers separately. Set aside. Peel and grate carrot. Put aside as well. In a pot, heat oil and sauté onion until soft. Add sweet banana peppers and sauté for a minute more. Add tomatoes, carrot, and tomato paste and sauté for another 1-2 minutes while stirring constantly. Pour in vegetable stock and cook for 5 minutes.

Wash and drain rice. Add rice, salt, pepper, and sugar to the soup and cook until rice is fully cooked, approx. 10 minutes. Finely chop parsley and stir in at the end. Serve hot.

SALADS

GARBANZO BEAN SALAD – *Nohut Salatası*

Serves 3-4   Difficulty level: easy

Prep time: 10 minutes

INGREDIENTS

13 oz. (400 g)	canned garbanzo beans (aka chickpeas)
⅞ cup (150 g)	canned corn
1	onion, red, medium-sized
1	red or yellow bell pepper
2	sweet banana peppers, green (*çarliston biberi*)
¼ bunch	parsley
¼ bunch	dill
1 Tbsp	pomegranate molasses (*nar ekşisi*)
3 Tbsp	olive oil
	salt

DIRECTIONS

Drain garbanzo beans and corn and put them into a mixing bowl.

Peel and dice onion. Wash bell pepper and sweet banana peppers, remove seeds, and dice into small cubes. Wash parsley and dill. Drain and finely chop.

Add all ingredients into the mixing bowl. Stir well and serve. This makes a great side to crispy rolls or crispy bagels, and don't forget the tea!

BEAN SALAD – *Piyaz*

Serves 3-4   Difficulty level: easy

Prep time: 15 minutes

INGREDIENTS

6½ cups (480 g)	canned white beans, drained
1	tomato, medium-sized
2	onions, medium-sized
½ bunch	fresh parsley
4 Tbsp	olive oil
2 Tbsp	vinegar
	juice of half a lemon
	salt
pinch	sugar

DIRECTIONS

Drain beans and put in a mixing bowl.

Peel tomato and cut into small cubes. Peel onions, halve and cut in thin strips or dice. Wash parsley, drain and finely chop. Add these to the mixing bowl.

Combine the rest of the ingredients to the beans and mix well. This is great as an appetizer too; traditionally part of the *meze* plate in kebab and fish restaurants.

BULGUR SALAD – *Kısır*

Serves 3-4

Prep time: 10 minutes

Difficulty level: easy

Resting time: 10 minutes

INGREDIENTS

1⅛ cups (250 g)	fine bulgur (*köftelik ince bulgur*)
	boiling water
3	green onions
¼ bunch	parsley
3-4 leaves	iceberg lettuce
3½ Tbsp	olive oil
1 Tbsp	tomato paste
1 Tbsp	red pepper paste, sweet (*tatlı biber salçası*)
1 tsp	salt
2 tsp	dried mint
½ tsp	black pepper
½ tsp	cumin, ground
½ tsp	paprika, sweet, ground
½ tsp	hot red pepper flakes (*pul biber*)
	juice of a lemon

DIRECTIONS

Put bulgur into a heat resistant mixing bowl that has a lid. Pour in boiling water until bulgur is completely immersed. Cover with lid and set aside for 10 minutes for it to absorb all the water.

In the meantime, wash green onions and remove stems. Cut into thin rings. Wash and drain parsley and finely chop. Wash iceberg lettuce and cut into small thin strips.

In a saucepan, heat oil and sauté tomato paste, and red pepper paste until fully combined and smooth.

Add all ingredients to the bulgur and mix well.

Afiyet olsun!

SHEPHERD'S SALAD – *Çoban Salatası*

Serves 2-3

Prep time: 10-15 minutes

Difficulty level: easy

INGREDIENTS

4	tomatoes, medium-sized
2	cucumbers, small-sized
2	thin green peppers, mild (*sivri biber*)
1	red or white onion, large-sized
¼ bunch	parsley
4 Tbsp	lemon juice
5 Tbsp	olive oil
	salt and pepper
	olives for garnish

DIRECTIONS

Peel tomatoes. Cut tomatoes and cucumbers into small, equal-sized cubes.

Wash and halve green peppers lengthwise, remove stem and seeds and cut into thin slices.

Peel onion, divide in half and cut into fine horizontal strips or dice.

 Wash and drain parsley and finely chop.

Combine all ingredients into a salad bowl and mix well.

Afiyet olsun!

RISONI/ORZO SALAD – *Arpa Şehriye Salatası*

Serves 3-4

Prep time: 10 minutes

Difficulty level: easy

Cooking time: about. 10 minutes

INGREDIENTS

1⅞ cups (400 g)	risoni/orzo (*arpa şehriye*)
3-4	baby pickles
1	carrot, large-sized
⅞ cup (150 g)	canned corn
1 cup (250 g)	vegan yogurt
1⅛ cups (250 g)	vegan mayonnaise
2 Tbsp	olive oil
	salt and pepper
½ tsp	hot red pepper flakes (*pul biber*)

DIRECTIONS

Cook risoni/orzo following directions on package, drain and run under cold water. Set aside and let cool.

Cut ends of baby pickles off and dice. Peel, wash, and grate carrot. Drain corn.

Combine all ingredients into a salad bowl and mix well.

Afiyet olsun!

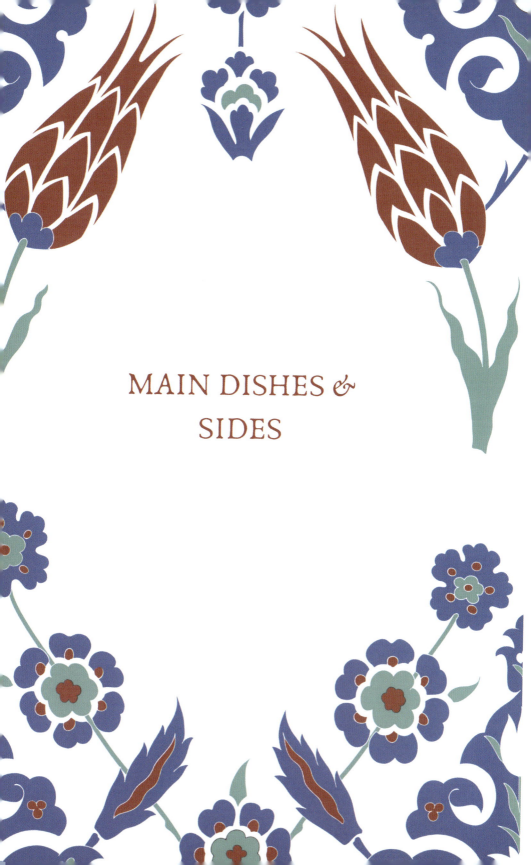

MAIN DISHES & SIDES

WHITE BEAN STEW – *Kuru Fasülye*

Serves 4-6

Difficulty level: easy

Prep time: 10-15 minutes
Cooking time: 1½ hours

Soaking time: 12 hours

INGREDIENTS

2 cups (400 g)	dry white beans
	water
	salt
2	onions, large-sized
1	garlic clove
1	carrot, large-sized
1	potato, large-sized
1	sweet banana pepper, green (*çarliston biberi*)
	oil for frying
1 Tbsp	tomato paste
1 Tbsp	red pepper paste, sweet (*tatlı biber salçası*)
3⅛ cups (750 ml)	vegetable stock
	black pepper
	hot red pepper flakes (*pul biber*) to taste

DIRECTIONS

Let beans sit in salted water overnight (minimum 12 hours). Then drain and put in a pot. Immerse beans completely in water and cook on medium heat for 30 minutes.

Peel onions, garlic, carrot and potato. Finely chop onions, garlic, and sweet banana pepper. Cut carrot into fine slices and dice the potato.

In another pot, sauté onions in oil for 2–3 minutes, then add garlic, banana pepper, tomato paste, and red pepper paste. Cook for another 2 minutes.

Drain beans and combine with vegetables in pot. Add potato, carrot, and vegetable stock. Add black pepper and hot red pepper flakes to taste. Cover and cook for about an hour on medium to low heat.

If you make this stew in a pressure cooker, then the cooking time goes down to 15–20 minutes.

This dish is traditionally served on a bed of rice (page 56) and a side of salad.

Afiyet olsun!

RUNNER BEAN STEW – *Taze Fasülye*

Serves 3-4

Prep time: 10 minutes

Difficulty level: easy

Cooking time: about 50 minutes

INGREDIENTS

3⅓ cups (500 g)	fresh runner beans (17.64 oz)
1	tomato, large-sized
1	potato, medium-sized
2	onions, medium-sized
1	garlic clove
1 tsp	salt
½ Tbsp	tomato paste
	hot red pepper flakes (*pul biber*) to taste
3½ Tbsp	olive oil
⅝ cup (150 ml)	water

DIRECTIONS

Wash and drain beans. Break the ends off by hand, no knife needed. Peel away the fibrous, unchewable strands if necessary. Then break beans by hand into bite-sized halves, or thirds. Put beans in a pot.

Peel and dice tomato, potato, onions, and garlic.

Add all ingredients to the pot and mix well until tomato paste is dissolved.

Cover and bring to a boil. Cook for 5 minutes on high heat, then turn down to low heat for 40 minutes.

Remove lid, raise heat and cook until most of the water has evaporated.

Serve warm or cold.

Afiyet olsun!

VEGETABLE STEW – *Türlü*

Serves 3-4

Prep time: 15 minutes

Cooking time: 20-30 minutes

Difficulty level: easy

Resting time: 15 minutes

INGREDIENTS

2	eggplants, medium-sized
2	potatoes, medium-sized
1	zucchini, medium-sized
2	tomatoes, medium-sized
1	bell pepper, red
6-7	fresh runner beans
1	onion, large-sized
2	garlic cloves
3 Tbsp	oil
1½ Tbsp	tomato paste
	water
	salt and pepper
	hot red pepper flakes (*pul biber*) to taste

DIRECTIONS

To make this dish visually more appealing dice all vegetables into equal-sized cubes.

Wash eggplants, trim the ends and partially remove the skin lengthwise every other inch (2 cm), leaving it striped with skin, as it were. Cut eggplant into small cubes and let them sit in a bowl of salted water for 15 minutes to remove the bitter taste. Drain water after 15 minutes.

Peel and dice potatoes, zucchini, and tomatoes. Wash and cut bell pepper into small cubes. Wash fresh runner beans, break ends off by hand and break in half.

Peel and dice onion and garlic cloves. In a pot, heat 3 Tbsp of oil and sauté onion and garlic together with tomato paste until soft. Add potatoes and cook for 3 minutes. Then add eggplants, zucchini, bell pepper, runner beans, tomatoes, salt, and pepper. Add hot red pepper flakes to taste. Mix well.

Add water until half of the vegetables are immersed. Cover pot and cook for 20 minutes or until soft. Serve hot.

Afiyet olsun!

LEEK STEW – *Pırasa Yemeği*

Serves 3-4   Difficulty level: easy

Prep time: 15 minutes   Cooking time: 20-30 minutes

This dish can be eaten warm or cold. The cold version has lemon juice instead of tomato paste and it is called *Zeytinyağlı Pırasa*, as pictured on page 72.

INGREDIENTS

2.2 lbs (1 kg)	leek
2	carrots, medium-sized
¼ cup (60 g)	rice
1	onion, large-sized
2	garlic cloves
5 Tbsp	olive oil
1 Tbsp	tomato paste (warm version)
½ cup (100 ml)	water
pinch	sugar
	salt and pepper
	lemon juice (cold version)

DIRECTIONS

Wash leeks. Remove roots and leaf ends together with fad-ed leaves. Slice leeks into thin rings and submerge in a bowl of cold water. Let them sit for a few minutes to soften any dirt. Scoop the leeks out into a colander and rinse thor-oughly.

Wash carrots and cut into thin slices. Wash rice, drain, and put aside.

Peel and dice onion and garlic and sauté in a pot with olive oil. Add tomato paste and cook for a few minutes until on-ions are soft. If you prefer to eat this dish cold in summer, omit the tomato paste. Stir in carrots and sauté for another 2 minutes. Add leek rings and rice, stir well. Finally, add water, sugar, salt, and pepper. Bring to boil and cook on low heat for about 20 minutes.

The vegetables should be soft, and the rice cooked. If you use a pressure cooker, then the cooking time goes down to about 10 to 12 minutes. Served hot in bowls as a main dish.

If you make the cold version of this dish put it on a platter and place in the middle of the table for self-serve. Drizzle with lemon juice.

Afiyet olsun!

WHITE CABBAGE STEW – *Kapuska*

Serves 3-4   Difficulty level: easy

Prep time: 10-15 minutes   Cooking time:35- 40 minutes

INGREDIENTS

2.2 lbs (1 kg)	white cabbage
1	red banana pepper, mild
3 Tbsp	coarse bulgur (*pilavlık bulgur*)
2	onions, medium-sized
2	garlic cloves
2 Tbsp	oil
1 Tbsp	tomato paste
1 tsp	red pepper paste, sweet (*tatlı biber salçası*)
2½ cups (600 ml)	boiling water
1 tsp	salt
	pepper
	hot red pepper flakes (*pul biber*) to taste
1 tsp	pomegranate molasses (*nar ekşisi*)

DIRECTIONS

Wash white cabbage and red banana pepper and cut into thin slices. Wash bulgur, drain, and set aside.

Peel and dice onions and garlic cloves. In a pot, heat oil and sauté onions and garlic until soft. Then add tomato paste and red pepper paste and cook for a few minutes. Add white cabbage and continue sautéing, stirring constantly. Cover and cook on low heat for 15 minutes.

Add boiling water, salt, pepper, and hot red pepper flakes to taste. Stir in bulgur and pomegranate molasses and bring to a boil.

Cover and let simmer on low heat for another 20 minutes. Served hot in bowls as a main dish.

Afiyet olsun!

ZUCCHINI STEW – *Kabak Yemeği*

Serves 3-4   Difficulty level: easy

Prep time: 10 minutes   Cooking time: 40 minutes

INGREDIENTS

2-3	zucchini, medium-sized
⅛ cup (30 g)	rice or coarse bulgur (*pilavlık bulgur*)
1	onion, medium-sized
1	garlic clove
2 Tbsp	oil
1 Tbsp	tomato paste
1¾ cups (400 ml)	boiling water
1 tsp	salt
	pepper
handful	fresh parsley and dill

DIRECTIONS

Peel zucchini, trim ends, wash and drain. Cut zucchini into even slices or cubes.

Wash rice (or bulgur), drain, and set aside.

Peel and dice onion and garlic. In a pot heat oil, sauté onion and garlic until soft. Add tomato paste and sauté for another minute. Then add zucchini and mix well.

Cover pot and cook on low heat for 7-8 minutes.

Add rice (or bulgur), boiling water, salt and pepper, and cook on low heat for 10 minutes more. Remove from heat.

Wash and finely chop fresh parsley and dill. Add to the stew and let rest for 2-3 minutes. Stir well and serve hot.

Afiyet olsun!

TURKISH RICE – *Pirinç Pilavı*

Serves 5-6

Prep time: 5-10 minutes

Resting time: 20-40 minutes

Difficulty level: easy

Cooking time: 20-30 minutes

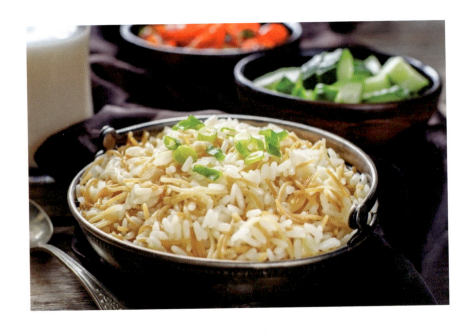

INGREDIENTS

1⅓ cups (300 g)	rice (*pilavlık pirinç*)
3 Tbsp	oil
⅜ cup (80 g)	risoni/orzo or capellini tagliati (*arpa şehriye* or *tel şehriye*)
2½ cups (600ml)	hot water
1 tsp	salt

Typical Turkish rice is made from the *Baldo* variety. It's a long grain rice grown in Turkey.

DIRECTIONS

Wash rice, drain, and let sit in salted lukewarm water for 20 minutes.

In a pot, heat oil and sauté risoni/orzo (or capellini tagliati) until golden to dark brown. Add rice and sauté for a few seconds more, stirring constantly. No more than 30 seconds.

Add hot water and salt and stir well. Make sure nothing is stuck to the bottom of the pot.

Bring rice to a boil, cover, and cook on low heat for 20-30 minutes. Do not stir during cooking time. Turn down heat completely and let the rice sit for another 10-20 minutes.

VARIATION: TOMATO RICE

This variation requires 2-3 peeled and grated tomatoes instead of risoni/orzo or capellini tagliati. Sauté grated tomatoes with oil and add the rice.

VARIATION: RICE WITH GARBANZO BEANS

Risoni/orzo or capellini tagliati is replaced with canned garbanzo beans (15.5 oz/439 g). Simply add the beans when adding the rice.

Afiyet olsun!

BULGUR RICE – *Bulgur Pilavı*

Serves 5-6

Difficulty level: easy

Prep time: 10 minutes

Cooking time: 15-20 minutes

INGREDIENTS

1⅓ cups (300 g)	coarse bulgur (*pilavlık bulgur*)
1	thin green pepper, mild (*sivri biber*)
1	potato, medium-sized
1	onion, large-sized
1	garlic clove
2 Tbsp	oil
1 Tbsp	tomato paste
3⅜ cups (800 ml)	hot water
1 tsp	salt
	pepper
½ tsp	paprika, sweet, ground
1 tsp	dried mint

DIRECTIONS

Wash bulgur, drain, and set aside. Wash thin green pepper, trim ends, remove seeds and cut into thin slices. Peel, wash, and dice potato.

Peel onion and garlic clove. Grate onion and mince garlic. In a pot, heat oil and sauté onion and garlic until soft. Add green pepper and tomato paste and cook for 2–3 minutes.

Now add bulgur and potato. Cook for a minute while stirring constantly. Add hot water, salt, pepper, and sweet paprika. Bring to a boil.

Cover and let simmer on low heat for 10–15 minutes until all the liquid is absorbed.

Served hot as a side dish sprinkled with dried mint.

Afiyet olsun!

ORIENTAL POTATOES – *Baharatlı Patates*

Serves 3-4

Prep time: 10 minutes

Difficulty level: easy

Baking time: 25-30 minutes

INGREDIENTS

3-4	potatoes, large-sized
2	garlic cloves
4 Tbsp	olive oil
½ tsp	salt
½ tsp	paprika, sweet, ground
1 tsp	thyme,
½ tsp	cumin
½ tsp	black pepper
	lemon juice

DIRECTIONS

Preheat oven to 390°F (200°C). Peel, wash, and cut potatoes into quarters and put into a mixing bowl. Peel garlic and put through a garlic press. Add all ingredients to the potatoes except the lemon juice. Mix well.

Spread potatoes on a baking sheet lined with parchment paper and bake for 25-30 minutes.

Sprinkle some lemon juice over the potatoes and serve hot.

Afiyet olsun!

COLD DISHES

OKRA STEW – *Bamya*

Serves 3-4

Difficulty level: easy

Prep time: 15 minutes

Resting time: 10 minutes

Cooking time: 30-35 minutes

INGREDIENTS

6¼ cups (600 g)	okra
3	tomatoes, large-sized
1	onion, medium-sized
5 Tbsp	olive oil
½ Tbsp	tomato paste
½ Tbsp	pepper paste, sweet (*tatlı biber salçası*)
1 tsp	salt
	juice of a lemon
½ tsp	sugar
1¼ cups (300 ml)	hot water
	hot red pepper flakes (*pul biber*) to taste

DIRECTIONS

Wash and rinse okra. Carefully sharpen the stems without cutting the okra itself, just as you would sharpen a pencil.

Put okra into a bowl of water. Add the juice of half a lemon and let sit for 10 minutes.

Peel and dice tomatoes and onion. In a pot, heat oil and sauté onion together with tomato paste and red pepper paste until onions are soft. Add tomatoes, cover and cook for 5 minutes.

Drain water out of okra bowl and put okra into the pot. Add salt, juice of half a lemon, sugar, and hot water. Stir once and cook over medium heat for 25–30 minutes.

This dish can be served warm or cold.

Afiyet olsun!

FAVA BEAN STEW – *Bakla*

Serves 3-4

Prep time: 10 minutes

Cooking time: 30-35 minutes

Difficulty level: easy

Resting time: 10 minutes

INGREDIENTS

17.6 oz (500 g)	fava (broad) bean pods, young
	cold water
	juice of half a lemon
1	onion, large-sized
5 Tbsp	olive oil
	hot water
1 tsp	salt
½ tsp	sugar
2	garlic cloves
handful	dill, fresh
6 Tbsp	vegan yogurt

DIRECTIONS

Wash fava bean pods in a bowl and drain. Trim ends and cut or break into 3 equal-sized pieces. Put bean pods into a bowl with cold water and lemon juice. Let sit for 10 minutes so that the bean pods keep their color during cooking.

In the meantime, peel and dice onion. In a saucepan, heat olive oil and sauté onion until soft. Drain bean pods and add them to the onions. Sauté as well for a few minutes. Then add hot water until the bean pods are half immersed in water. Stir in salt and sugar. Cover and cook over medium heat for 30-35 minutes. If you use a pressure cooker, then the cooking time goes down to about 15 minutes.

Peel garlic cloves and either use a garlic press or mince. Mix garlic with vegan yogurt and salt as needed.

Wash and chop dill. Put the bean pods on a serving plate and cover with fresh dill.

Serve cold topped with a spoonful of garlic yogurt.

Afiyet olsun!

THE IMAM FAINTED – *Imam Bayıldı*

Serves 5-6

Prep time: 10 minutes

Frying time: 20 minutes

Difficulty level: moderate

Resting time: 30 minutes

Baking time: 25-30 minutes

INGREDIENTS

6	eggplants, medium-sized
4	thin green peppers, mild (*sivri biber*)
4	tomatoes, medium-sized
6	onions, medium-sized
4-5	garlic cloves
	olive oil
	salt and pepper
pinch	sugar
1 Tbsp	tomato paste
1 cup (250 ml)	hot water

DIRECTIONS

Peel 3-4 strips off eggplants lengthwise. Let striped egg-plants sit in saltwater for 15-20 minutes.

Wash thin green peppers. Trim ends, remove seeds, and cut into small pieces. Peel and dice tomatoes.

Peel onions and garlic cloves. Cut onions in half then cut lengthwise into fine strips. Dice garlic.

In a frying pan, heat oil and sauté onions and garlic over medium heat for 5 minutes until soft. Add green peppers and sauté for another 2 minutes. Add tomatoes, salt, pepper, and sugar. Cook for another 2 minutes then remove from heat.

Preheat oven to 360°F (180°C). Pat dry eggplants. In a frying pan heat sufficient oil and fry eggplants evenly on all sides until soft and slightly browning. Place the fried eggplants on paper towel to remove excess oil. Set eggplants into a rectangular casserole dish. Slice lengthwise down the middle of the eggplant. Pull the sides apart and slightly flatten. This creates a pocket, fill pocket with the onion mixture.

Dissolve tomato paste in hot water. Spoon this liquid on and around the eggplants until it is used up.

Bake for 25-30 minutes. Allow to completely cool before serving.

Afiyet olsun!

VEGETABLE RAGOUT – *Şakşuka*

Serves 4-5

Difficulty level: easy

Prep time: 15 minutes

Resting time: 15 minutes

Baking time: 25-30 minutes

Cooking time: 5-10 minutes

INGREDIENTS

3	eggplants, medium-sized
1	zucchini, large-sized
2	carrots
6	sweet banana peppers, green (*çarliston biberi*)
1	red or yellow bell pepper
6-7	tomatoes, medium-sized
2	garlic cloves
½ cup (100 ml)	olive oil
	salt

DIRECTIONS

Peel 3-4 strips off eggplants lengthwise. Let striped egg-plants sit in saltwater for 15-20 minutes.

Peel zucchini and carrots. Cut lengthwise and slice into half inch slices (1 cm). Wash sweet banana peppers and bell pepper, remove seeds, and cut into pieces no bigger than one inch (2 cm).

Peel tomatoes and either dice or grate. Peel garlic cloves and either mince or press.

Preheat oven to 360°F (180°C). Drain and dice eggplants. Add to a bowl together with zucchini, carrots, peppers, and olive oil. Salt to taste and mix well. Place vegetables onto a baking sheet lined with parchment paper and bake for 25-30 minutes, flipping and mixing vegetables halfway through.

In a frying pan mix tomatoes, garlic, and salt and cook until it thickens and becomes a sauce.

Place vegetables onto a serving plate and pour tomato sauce on top.

Serve warm or cold.

Afiyet olsun!

STUFFED PEPPERS – *Biber Dolması*

Serves 5-10   Difficulty level: moderate

Prep time: 40 minutes   Cooking time: 50-60 minutes

INGREDIENTS

10	small green (bell-like) peppers with <u>thin</u> skin (*dolmalık biber*)
1 cup (240 g)	rice
2 Tbsp	currants (*kuş üzümü*)
5	cherry tomatoes
2	tomatoes, medium-sized
¼ bunch	fresh parsley
6	onions, medium-sized
	olive oil
2 Tbsp	pine nuts
	water
1 tsp	salt
1 tsp	pepper
½ tsp	sugar
1 Tbsp	dried mint
½ tsp	allspice, ground (*yenibahar*)

DIRECTIONS

Wash green peppers, carefully cut out stem, and remove seeds. Wash rice, drain, and set aside. Wash currants, drain, and set aside. Wash cherry tomatoes, cut into halves and set aside.

Peel and dice tomatoes. Wash and finely chop parsley and set aside as well.

Peel and dice onions. In a saucepot, heat oil and sauté onions until soft. Lower heat and add rice and pine nuts, continue sautéing for 5 minutes, stirring constantly. Add tomatoes and currants and cook for another 3–4 minutes, stirring constantly. Add ⅞ cup (200 ml) water and let simmer for 3–5 minutes. Remove from heat. Add salt, pepper, sugar, dried mint, chopped parsley, and allspice. Mix well.

Using a teaspoon, stuff peppers with rice mixture, leaving half an inch (1 cm) room at the top. The rice will fill the gap when cooked. Place half a cherry tomato on each stuffed pepper. Set peppers upright and side by side into a high pot, leaving no room between peppers, making sure they do not fall over. Add water until peppers are half immersed. Cover pot and bring to a boil. Reduce heat and cook for 30–40 minutes or until rice is cooked.

COLD LEEK STEW – *Zeytinyağlı Pırasa*

You can find this recipe on page 50. For the cold version – as seen in this picture – the tomato paste is omitted. Lemon juice is sprinkled on top of the dish instead when served.

Afiyet olsun!

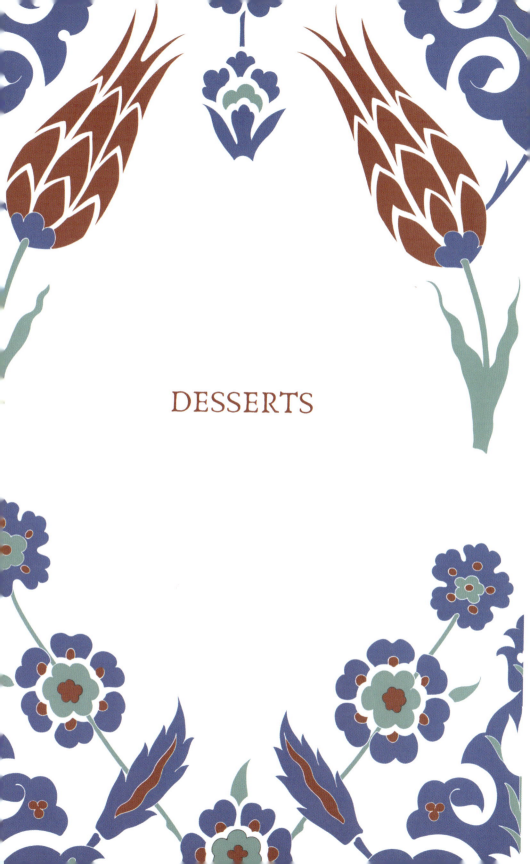

DESSERTS

CANDIED PUMPKIN – *Kabak Tatlısı*

Serves 3–4

Prep time: 10 minutes

Cooking time: ~50 minutes

Difficulty level: easy

Resting time: 1 hour

INGREDIENTS

21.2 oz (600 g)	kabocha squash or Japanese pumpkin (*balkabağı*)
1 cup (200 g)	sugar
½ cup (100 ml)	water
⅜ cup (50 g)	walnuts, coarsely chopped
	grape syrup (*pekmez*, alternatively any other type of molasses will do)

DIRECTIONS

Halve and peel pumpkin, scoop out seeds with a spoon. Cut pumpkin into equal bite-sized pieces, approximately an inch wide and an inch thick (2 cm x 2 cm). Wash pieces thoroughly and place into a saucepot. Sprinkle with sugar. Cover and let sit for an hour. This process unlocks the sweet pumpkin juice.

Add water and cook covered on medium heat for 50 minutes.

Set pumpkin pieces onto a serving plate and sprinkle with coarsely chopped walnuts.

To add more sweetness, you can drizzle grape syrup, or your molasses of choice, onto the pumpkin pieces.

TIP

Experience a variation with a drizzle of sesame paste (*tahini*) over the pumpkin pieces instead of grape syrup.

This dessert tastes best when served warm.

Afiyet olsun!

SEMOLINA HALVA – *Irmik Helvası*

Serves 3-4

Difficulty level: easy

Prep time: 5 minutes

Cooking time: 10 minutes

INGREDIENTS

1 cup (200 g)	sugar
1⅜ cups (330 ml)	water
½ cup (100 ml)	oil
¾ cup (160 g)	semolina *(irmik)*
⅛ cup (25 g)	pine nuts
	vegan ice cream

DIRECTIONS

Dissolve sugar in water and set aside.

In a saucepan, heat oil, add semolina and pine nuts and sauté until pine nuts are golden brown and semolina golden yellow, stirring constantly. This can take a few minutes.

Add sugar water to saucepan carefully, stirring constantly. Bring to a boil and keep stirring until semolina becomes firm.

Set saucepan aside and allow it to cool down.

Cover the inside of four small bowls with plastic wrap. Fill half of each bowl with halva, place a spoonful of vegan ice cream in the middle, then fill the rest of the bowl with halva. Place a dessert plate face down on top of the bowl. Carefully flip it over. Pulling gently on the plastic wrap, lift the small bowl off, leaving a nicely formed halva. Serve immediately. Warm halva will melt the ice cream so that you experience a lava effect. Maybe this dessert should be called ha-*lava*...

TIP

Sprinkle a dash of ground cinnamon on top when preparing this dessert in winter.

Afiyet olsun!

SEMOLINA CAKE – *Revani*

Serves 3–4

Difficulty level: easy

Prep time: 10 minutes

Resting time: 10–15 minutes

Cooking time: 10 minutes

Baking time: 30–35 minutes

DOUGH INGREDIENTS

1 tub (500 g)	vegan yogurt, 16.3 fl. oz.
1 tub	flour
1 tub	semolina (*irmik*)
1 tub	sugar
1 tub	oil + more for greasing
1 Tbsp	baking powder
1 Tbsp	vanilla sugar
3 Tbsp	sparkling water
1 Tbsp	grated lemon zest
1 Tbsp	lemon juice
	shredded coconut and ground pistachios for garnish

SYRUP INGREDIENTS

1¼ cups (250 g)	sugar
⅝ cup (150 ml)	water
1 tsp	lemon juice

DIRECTIONS

In a saucepan add sugar, water, and lemon juice. Bring to a

boil and let simmer on low heat for 10 minutes. Set the syrup aside and allow it to cool.

Preheat oven to 390°F (200°C). Pour vegan yogurt into a large mixing bowl and use the same yogurt tub to measure out and add each of the following ingredients: flour, semolina, sugar, and oil. Also add baking powder, vanilla sugar, sparkling water, grated lemon zest and lemon juice — but not using the tub! Mix well.

Pour batter evenly into a greased casserole dish and bake for 30-35 minutes until crust is caramel brown.

Let cake cool for 10-15 minutes, then pour lukewarm syrup evenly on top. It will be absorbed in a few minutes.

Cut cake into small rectangular pieces and sprinkle with shredded coconut and ground pistachios. This cake tastes best when eaten the next day.

PHYLLO PASTRY DESSERT – *Baklava*

Serves 6-8

Difficulty level: easy

Prep time: 25-20 minutes
Cooking time: 10 minutes

Resting time: 20 minutes
Baking time: 20-25 minutes

DOUGH INGREDIENTS

⅞ cup (150 g)	hazelnuts, chopped
⅞ cup (100 g)	almonds, blanched and chopped
	oil for greasing
17.6 oz (500 g)	phyllo pastry sheets (*baklavalık yufka*)

SYRUP INGREDIENTS

1 cup (200 g)	sugar
⅝ cup (150 ml)	water
½ cup (125 ml)	agave syrup (instead of honey)
	juice of half a lemon

DIRECTIONS

In a saucepan add water, sugar, agave syrup, and lemon juice. Bring to a boil, stirring constantly. Lower heat and let simmer for about 10 minutes. Then set aside and let syrup cool down.

Mix chopped hazelnuts and almonds in a separate bowl.

Grease a casserole dish and preheat oven to 360°F (180°C). Cut the phyllo sheets to the size of the casserole dish. Lay 6 sheets into the form individually, brushing oil on each one before stacking the next. After oiling the top sheet, spread the nut mixture evenly over it. Then add another 6 sheets, again oiling as you stack. With a sharp knife cut the baklava into diamond shaped pieces, 3 inches by 2 inches (6 cm x 4 cm). Then place in oven for 20-25 minutes or until golden brown.

Gently pour cooled syrup onto hot baklava and let sit for a whole day to allow syrup to be absorbed. Enjoy this classic!

Afiyet olsun!

SHREDDED PHYLLO DESSERT – *Kadayıf*

Serves 6–8

Difficulty level: easy

Prep time: 15 minutes

Cooking time: 10 minutes

Baking time: 25–30 minutes

DOUGH INGREDIENTS

17.6 oz (500 g)	shredded phyllo (*tel kadayıf*)
1⅛ cups (250 g)	vegan margarine
⅞ cup (50 g)	almonds, blanched, finely chopped
⅜ cup (50 g)	walnuts, finely chopped
	minced pistachios for garnish

SYRUP INGREDIENTS

1¾ cups (400 ml)	water
2½ cups (500 g)	sugar
	juice of half a lemon

DIRECTIONS

Into a saucepan add water, sugar, and lemon juice. Bring to a boil while stirring constantly. Lower heat and let simmer for about 10 minutes. Set aside and let syrup cool.

Remove shredded phyllo dough from packaging. Pull and loosen apart with your hands and place it into a large bowl. Preheat oven to 390°F (200°C). Melt vegan margarine and pour evenly onto the shredded phyllo. Take half of the phyllo dough and press into a large casserole dish, making an even, flat layer. Spread chopped walnuts and almonds uniformly over the phyllo dough.

Add the other half of the dough to the casserole dish and press gently to flatten the dough out into an even top layer. Bake for 25–30 minutes until golden brown.

Cut hot phyllo pastry into desired shape (usually rectangles or triangles) with a sharp knife. Pour syrup on top, covering the entire dessert. Let sit a few hours up to a day before serving.

Decorate with ground pistachios and serve.

Afiyet olsun!

NOAH'S PUDDING – *Aşure*

Serves 8-10

Prep time: 15-20 minutes

Cooking time: 1½ hours

Difficulty level: moderate

Resting time: 20-22 hours
.

INGREDIENTS

¾ cup (150 g)	barley (*aşurelik buğday*)
	water
¼ cup (50 g)	dry garbanzo beans
¼ cup (50 g)	dry white beans
⅓ cup (60 g)	dried apricots, finely diced
⅜ cup (60 g)	dried figs, finely diced
⅜ cup (60 g)	sultana or alternatively raisins
1 cup (200 g)	sugar

GARNISH, TO TASTE

walnuts

currants (*kuş üzümü*)

hazelnuts

cinnamon, ground

pistachios, ground

pomegranate arils

pine nuts

DIRECTIONS

Wash and rinse barley and combine with a quart (1 L) of water in a large pot that has a capacity of at least a gallon (4 L). Cover barley and let sit in water for 10-12 hours. Then bring to boil and turn heat down completely. Let sit covered for another 10 hours.

Soak garbanzo beans and white beans simultaneously, yet separately for 10 hours in sufficient water, then drain. In separate saucepans, add garbanzo beans and white beans. Add enough water to cover beans, bring to a boil and let simmer on low heat for an hour until beans are cooked. Drain and discard water.

Put apricots, figs, and sultana (or raisins), each separately into its own saucepan. Add enough water to each saucepan to cover its respective ingredient. Bring to a boil, then discard water. This step prevents the pudding from becoming dark.

Add to the barley pot in this exact order: garbanzo beans, white beans, apricots, figs, and sultana (or raisins). Do not stir. Slowly add a quart (1 L) of water and, again, do not stir when bringing to a boil. Then let simmer on medium heat for 10 minutes. Now you can stir the pot, cooking for another 5 minutes. Add sugar, mix well and turn down heat completely.

As soon as the pudding has cooled down, dish out into little dessert bowls. Decorate with walnuts, currants, hazelnuts, and any other garnish ingredient you have at hand.

ABOUT *Aşure*

Aşure is the most famous vegan dessert on the Turkish menu. Legend has it that Noah cooked this pudding with the leftover food on the Ark after it landed. Since the ingredients consist of leftovers, there is no typical *Aşure* recipe. The main point is to check what is available at home and to gather at least 7-10 ingredients to make *Aşure*.

Since preparing this dessert takes a lot of time, it is not worth it to make in small batches. In turn, with such a large amount it is customary to share *Aşure* with neighbors, friends, and family. It is said to strengthen community ties and raise one's honor.

Afiyet olsun!

DRIED FRUIT COMPOTE – *Hoşaf*

Serves 3-4   Difficulty level: easy

Prep time: 10 minutes   Resting time: 6-12 hours
Cooking time: 20 minutes

INGREDIENTS

1 cup (150 g)	sultana (or raisins)
½ cup (95 g)	dried apricots, whole
½ cup (65 g)	dried prunes, whole
6½ cups (1.4L)	water + more to soak
1 cup (200 g)	sugar
1	cinnamon stick
2	cloves

DIRECTIONS

Wash dried fruit. Cut each of the apricots and prunes — depending on the size — into two or four pieces and let soak overnight in water together with the sultana (or raisins).

Drain fruit water and transfer fruit to a pot. Add the water, stir, and bring to a boil. Let simmer for 15 minutes.

Add sugar, cinnamon stick, and cloves. Mix well and simmer for another 5 minutes. If you want the compote to be less sweet, simply reduce the sugar.

Pour *Hoşaf* into small bowls and serve cold. It is popular in meals where rice is the side dish, having an occasional spoonful during the main course.

DISCLAIMER

The author put forth her best effort to make this book a reality by bringing these recipes together. The information herein, i.e. the ingredients, suggestions, and directions are guidelines only. Different appliance brands, wattages, and temperatures will lead to slightly different outcomes. We recommend fully reading a recipe before starting it and to always use your best judgement. We disavow any and all responsibility for any and all adverse effects resulting from the use or misuse of the information provided in this book.

Neither the publisher nor the author is responsible for any adverse reaction to the ingredients contained in this book. Nor are they responsible for your specific health or allergy needs that may require medical supervision.

If you have any questions, comments, or just want to say hi, send an email to sd.international.inc@gmail.com.

Thank you

NOTES

Printed in Great Britain
by Amazon